DRAW IT!

SEA LIFE

BECKY J. RADTKE

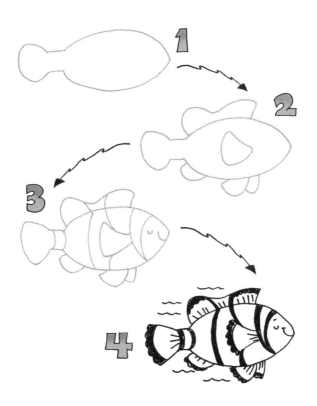

DOVER PUBLICATIONS, INC.
Mineola, New York

Bibliographical Note

Draw It! Sea Life is a new work, first published by Dover
Publications, Inc., in 2013.

International Standard Book Number
ISBN-13: 978-0-486-49958-1
ISBN-10: 0-486-49958-8

Manufactured in the United States by Courier Corporation
49958801   2013
www.doverpublications.com

Note

Would you like to draw fish and other sea creatures? In this handy book, you'll learn how to draw a dogfish, a lobster, a sea turtle, and many, many more animals that live in the sea. Just follow the steps, from 1 to 4. Step 1 shows you the basic shape. Step 2 might add fins and a tail. By Step 3, you will see the entire creature. Step 4 shows you how to add details such as spots or stripes to finish your picture. Opposite each page with the four drawing steps is another page where you can draw your sea creature. There's even a helpful hint for each picture!

Angelfish

This triangular beauty can be found in South America and many aquariums!

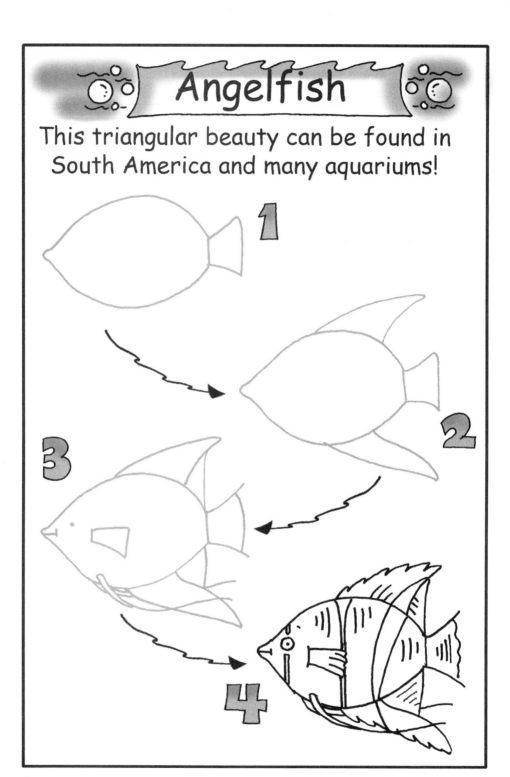

Blowfish

Also called a puffer, it swallows
lots of water to take on a round shape.

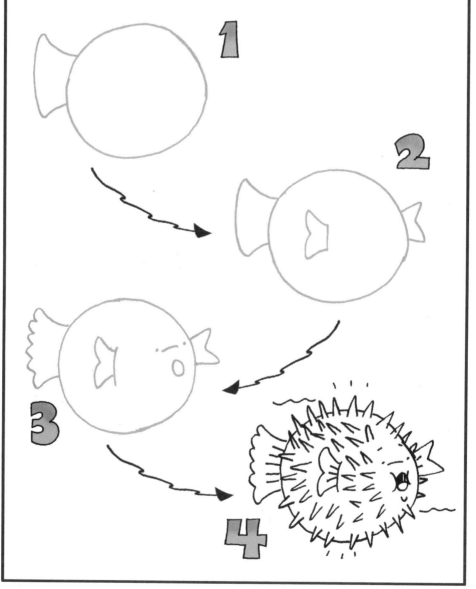

Blue Whale

Happy in any ocean, this giant makes
sounds that travel for hundreds of miles.

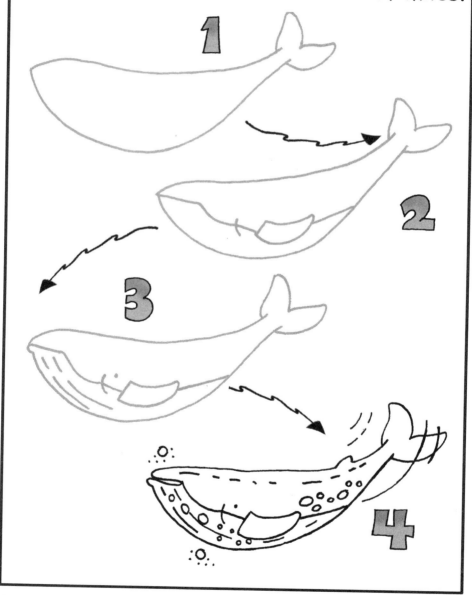

Clam

Clams range in size from a few inches to several feet!

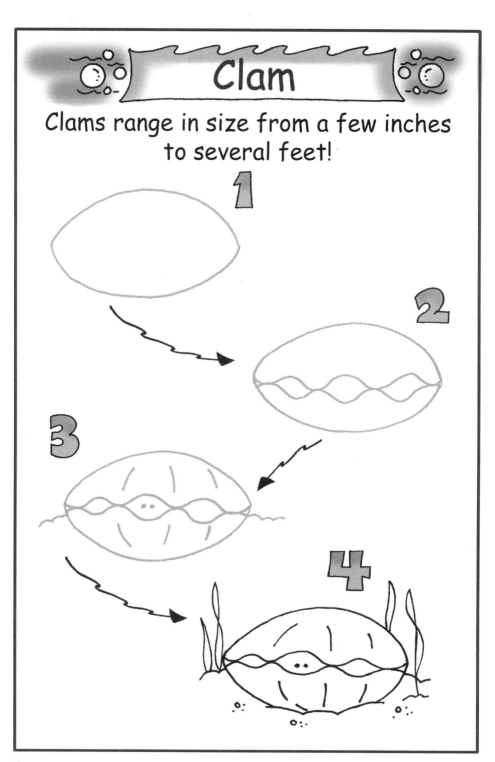

Clownfish

Wildly popular, this colorful fish is a poor swimmer that doesn't go far.

Crab

This clawed creature walks sideways,
due to the way its legs bend.

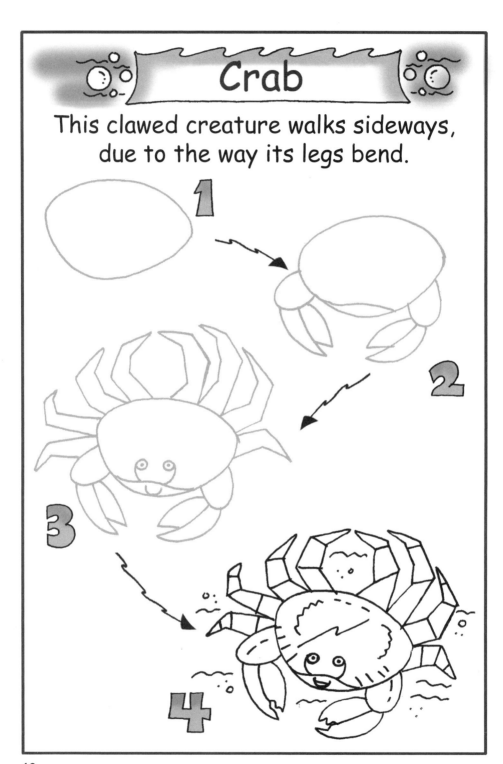

Dogfish

This small shark's egg cases, found on beaches, are called "mermaid's purses."

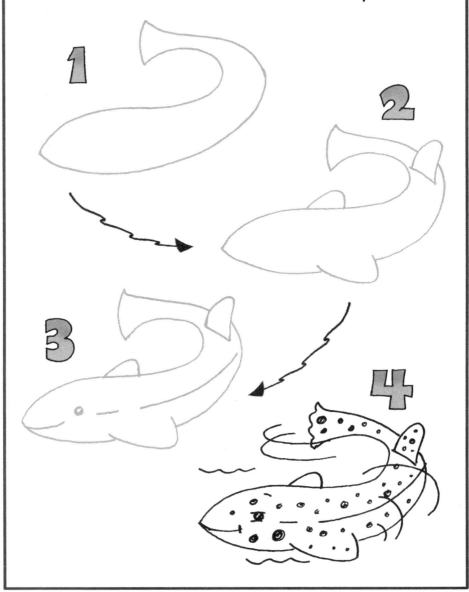

Dolphin

These marine mammals are very smart and enjoy dining on squid and fish.

Electric Eel

This snakelike hunter zaps its prey with huge electrical charges.

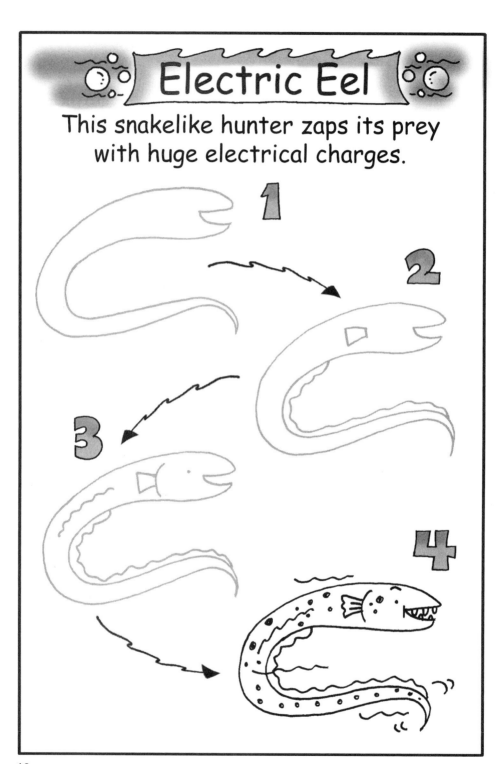

Fin Whale

Super sleek, this fellow has a dorsal fin on his back.

Flounder

Lying flat on the sandy sea floor lets this fish catch its prey by surprise.

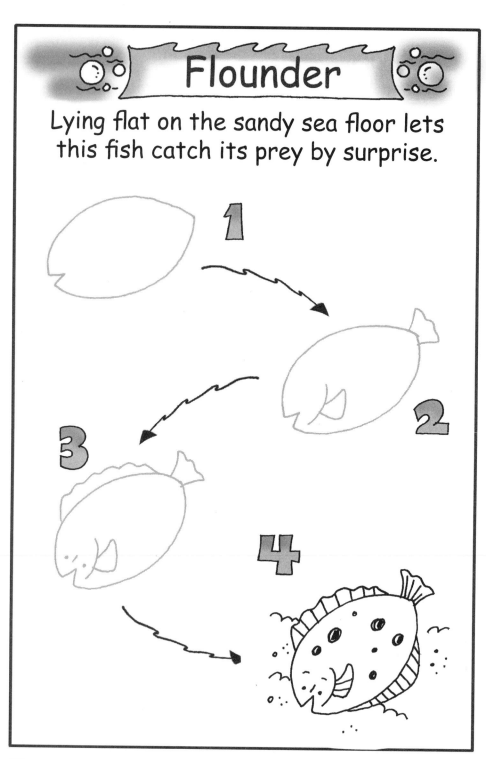

Great White Shark

With its sharp teeth, this predator is at the top of the oceanic food chain.

Hammerhead Shark

This odd-looking creature has special head sensors to help it locate food.

Humpback Whale

This whopper has a huge, powerful tail that it slaps on the water's surface.

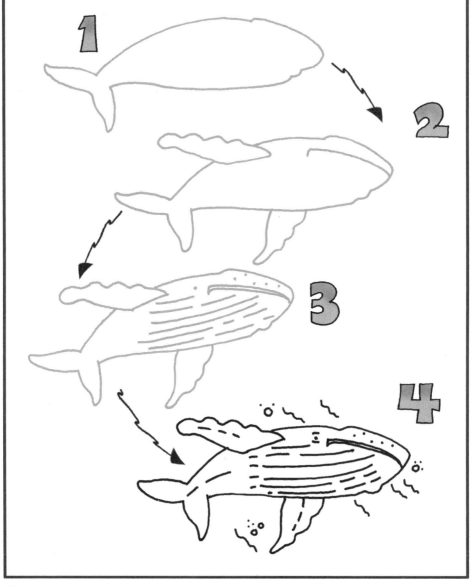

Jellyfish

This ocean resident has tentacles that sting.

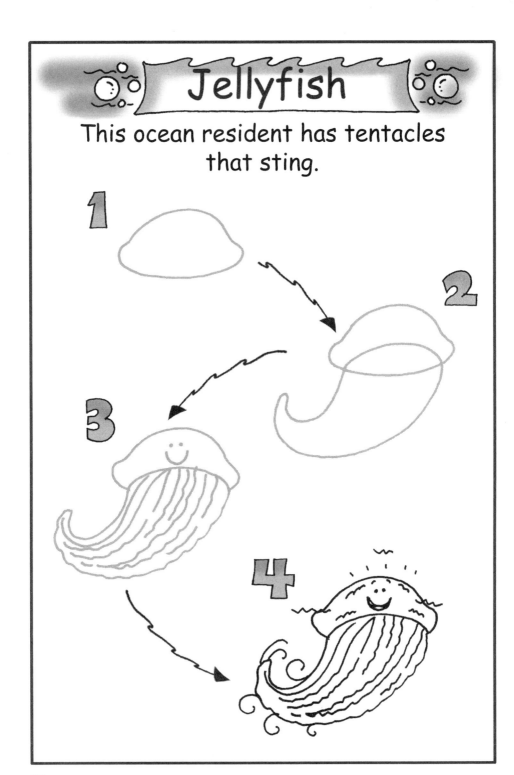

Killer Whale

The largest of the dolphin species,
this whale lives in a pod (family group).

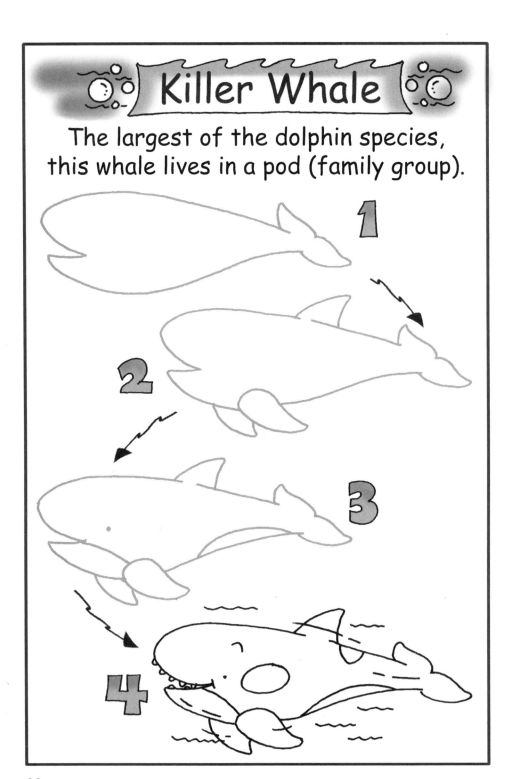

Lantern Fish

This deep-sea oddity has its own system of producing light.

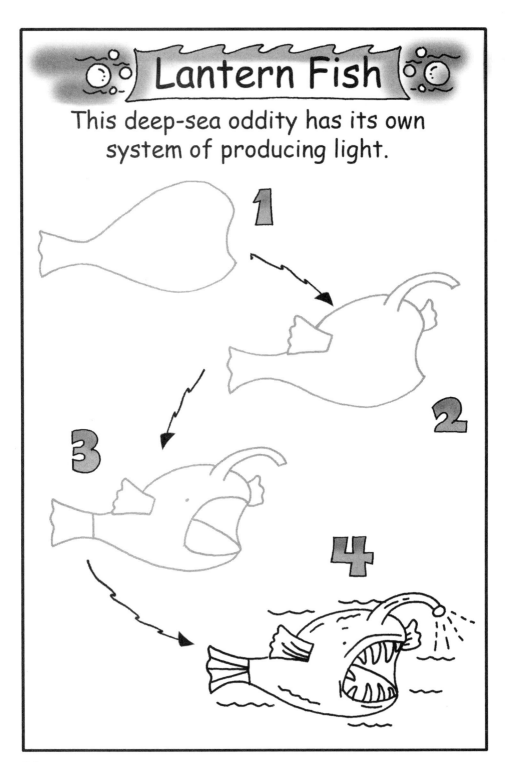

Lion Fish

Also known as a turkey fish, this spiny being is venomous.

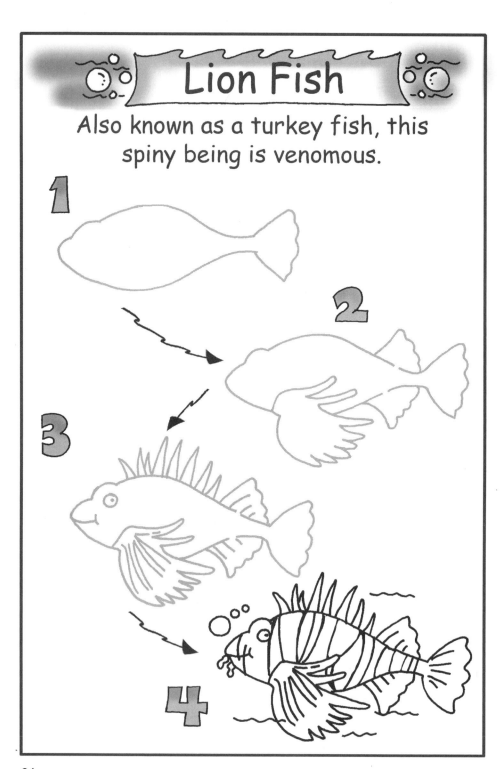

Lobster

This crustacean can shed its skeleton!

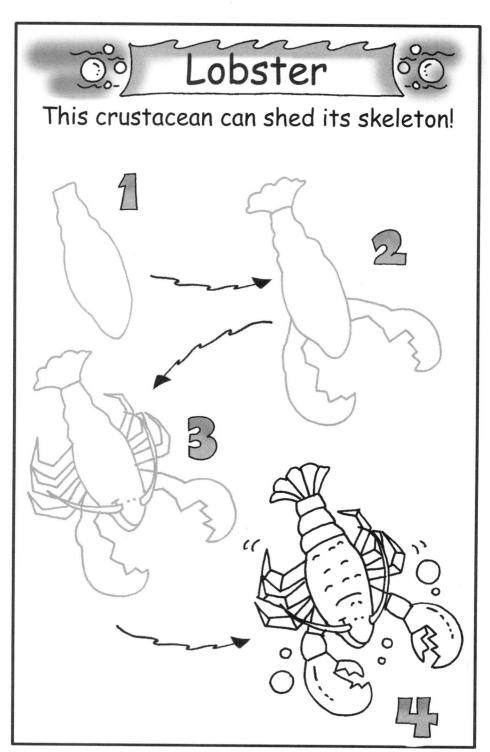

Manatee

Referred to as a sea cow, this gentle mammal must come up regularly for air.

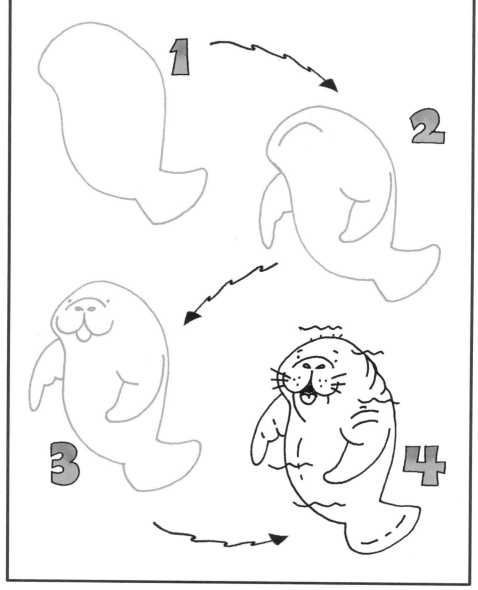

Manta Ray

This toothless creature can grow to over twenty-five feet.

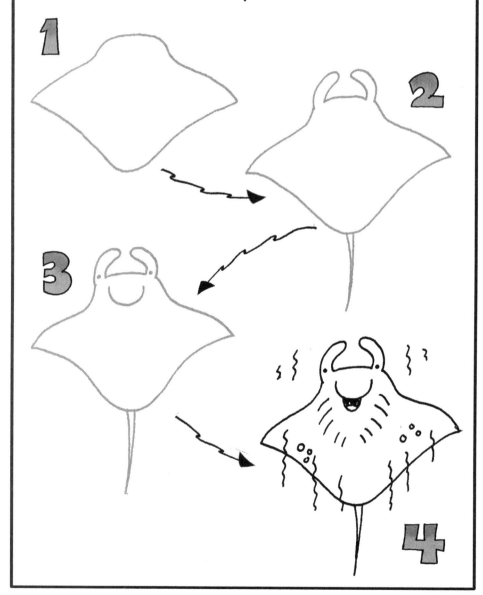

Marlin

With a spear-shaped bill, this fish will fight if it is caught.

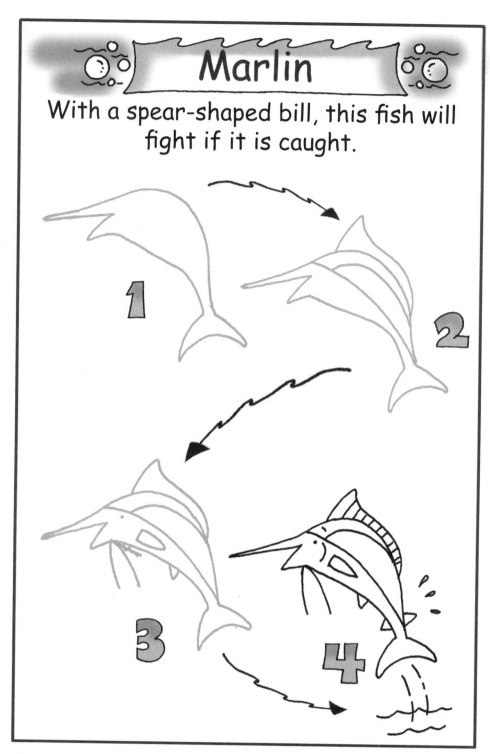

Narwhal

This whale species is called the unicorn of the sea.

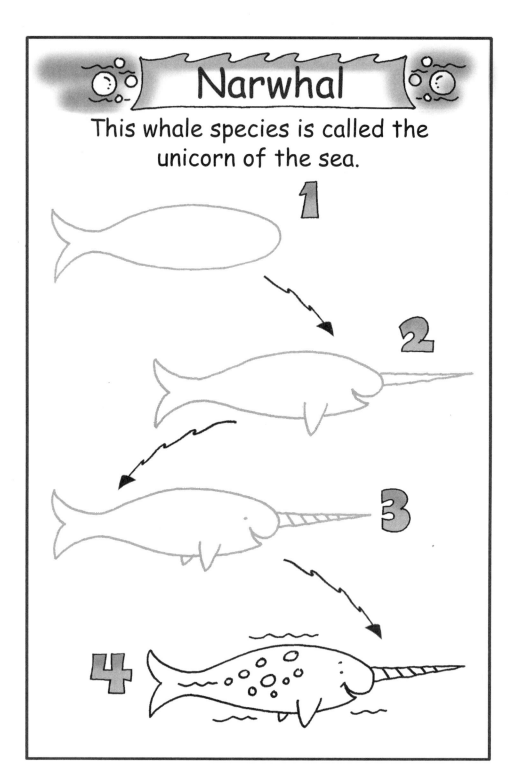

Nurse Shark

Found in warm, shallow water, this slowpoke does its hunting at night.

49

Octopus

Its boneless body includes eight arms with suction cups on their undersides.

Oyster

When danger calls, this mollusk uses its strong muscles to shut its shell.

This peaceful fish changes colors depending on how the light reflects off it.

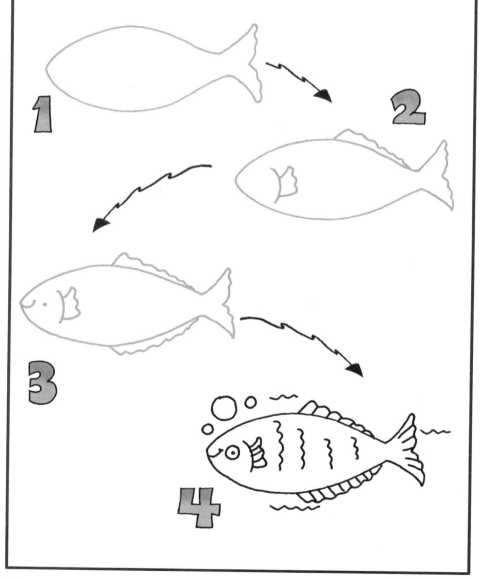

Seal

This webbed-foot mammal keeps warm
with its fur and a layer of blubber.

Sea Gull

Mimicking sounds of rain by stamping its feet, this bird tricks worms to come out.

Sea Horse

To stay put when it rests, this bony fish can curl its tail around seaweed!

Sea Otter

This very clean critter sleeps while floating on its back.

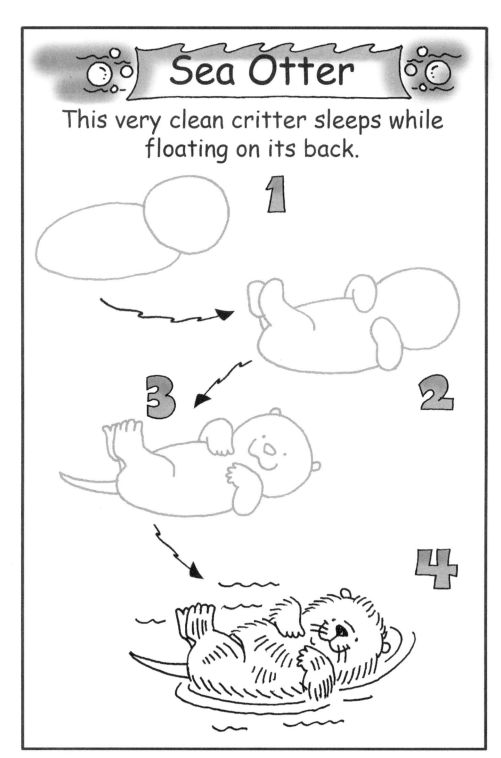

Sea Turtle

It's interesting that this fellow is unable to pull its head and legs inside its shell.

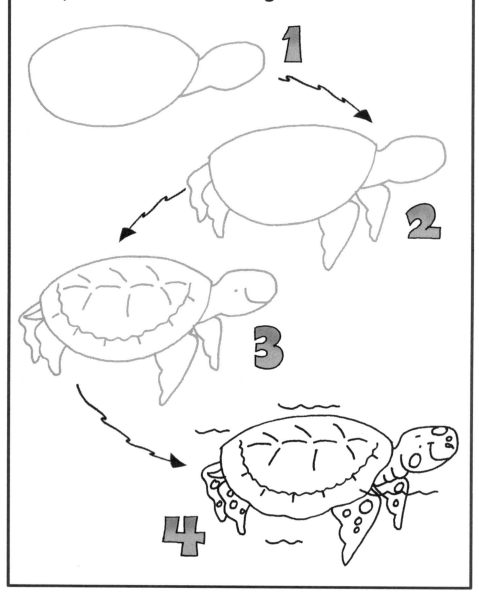

Shrimp

This jointed-legged crustacean lives in a school with others.

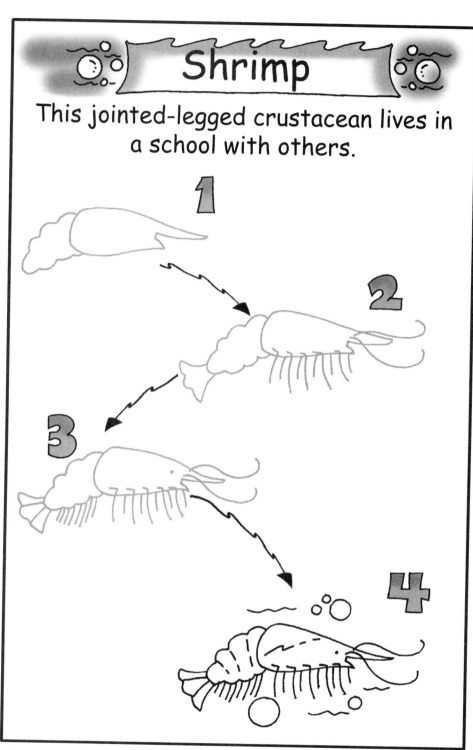

Squid

After stalking its prey, this soft-bodied animal makes the capture with its arms.

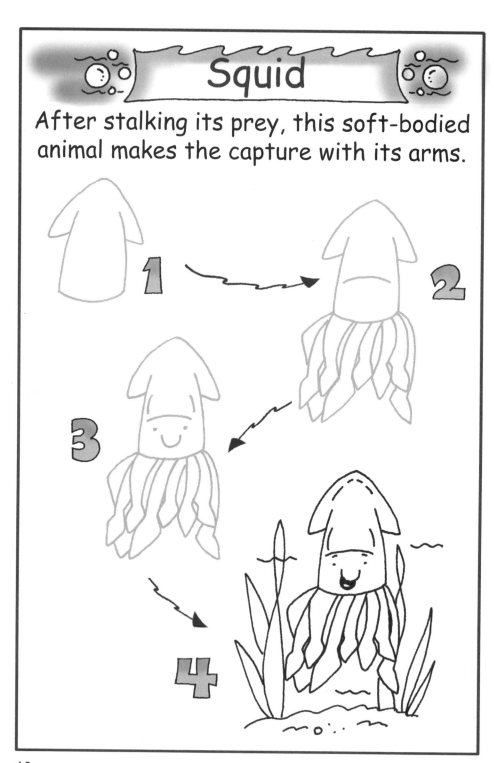

Starfish

If an arm is lost, it has the amazing ability to grow one back!

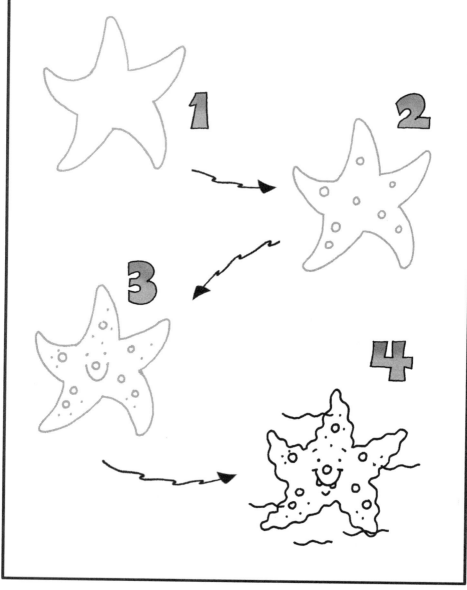

Swordfish

It uses its swordlike bill to deter enemies.

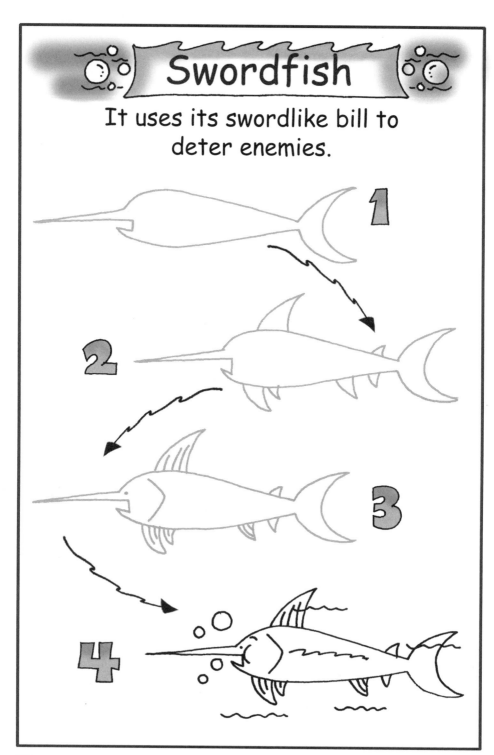

Tiger Shark

Named for its stripes, this blunt-nosed scavenger is extremely dangerous.

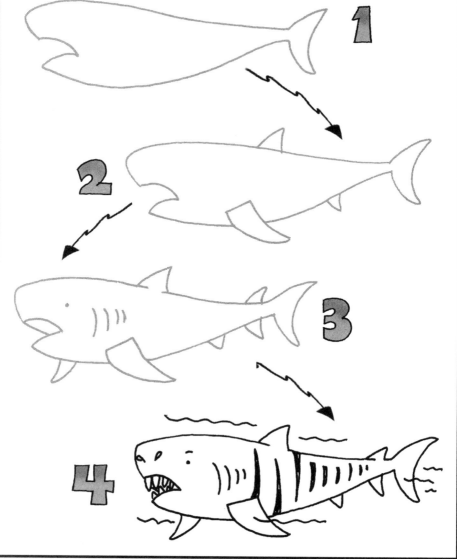

Walrus

This sea animal breaks holes in the ice with its tusks for breathing.

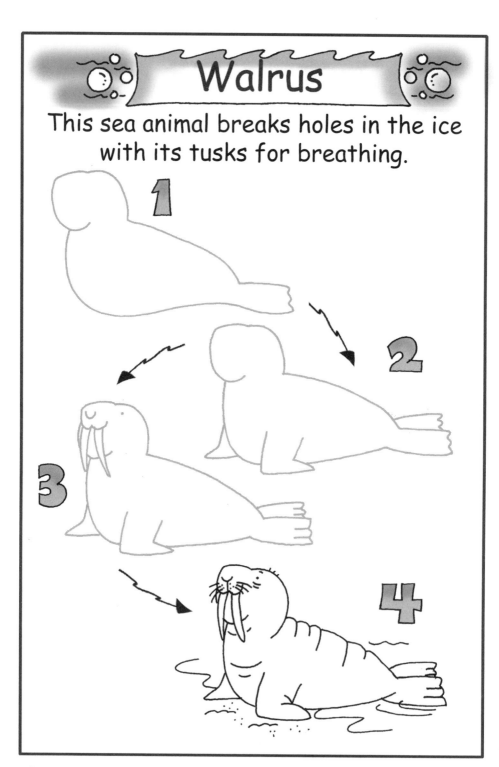